I0027181

Writing!
to WOW!

Praise for

Writing to WOW!

"Susie Augustin published, edited and coached me through my #1 Bestselling book *Getting Your Life to a 10 Plus*, and two books I co-authored. She is focused, savvy, creative and patient, and inspires such unique ideas for writing and branding through books, and being an author. I am positively hiring her again for my next book and going through her coaching programs."
~ **Kim Somers Egelsee**, Life Coach, Confidence Expert, Speaker, #1 Bestselling Author of *Getting Your Life to a 10 Plus*

"Susie Augustin is certainly an expert in her field as a book coach, editor and guide. She engages with passion for each author's project, provides direction and a clear-cut plan to achieve your dreams. On the day I shared my ideas for my next book, she was totally on the same page with me and I believe she wanted me to have an amazing book as badly as I did. She was there every step of the way...knowing exactly what I need and pushing me to stay on course. Thank you Susie, we accomplished not only one book on this journey, but two at the same time and you made sure they were all bestsellers. I highly recommend Susie, she will make your dream a reality."
~ **Claudia Cooley**, Radio Show Host,
#1 Bestselling Author of *Savvy Women Revving Up for Success*

"Susie inspired me to follow my dream of writing my own book and assisted me in downloading my 30 plus years of experience into this project! Her enthusiasm, creativity, passion, and tenacity inspires me to stay focused and to meet my goals necessary for a successful launch! She made what would seem to be a arduous task seem fun, exciting and motivating!"
~ **Karla Keene,** CEO Clarity Clinical Skincare, Inc.,
Author of *Your Esthetics Coach*

"Susie is patient, kind, and compassionate while unyielding in moving you forward toward attaining your conceptual dream of book writing. She is energetic and positive, even when you are not. Her intuitive nature allows for her to accurately process your aspirations, crafting it in such a way as to guide you pen to paper. While writing is personally draining and stimulating all in one breath, Susie's steady hand maintains your focus, feeding your creativity while you reach for the stars!"
~ **Tracy Rath,** Founder of OC's Hair Police
#1 Bestselling Author of *Louse Out*

"WOW! Susie is a true gift to writers. She helped shape and support my vision without taking it over. From the early pages to the final book cover, she is a mentor and guide with exceptional skill. I am grateful to have partnered with her on this publishing journey!"
~ **Liz Rosado-McGrath,** MEd, Founder of Transformed Teachers,
Author of *From Burned Out to Fired Up: Teachers Reignite Their Passion to Inspire*

"Giving a huge thumbs up for *Writing to Wow!* Why? Susie Augustin writes in a concise format that I personally feel is the way 95% of most people learn...Step by step! It truly is how I personally take things in! You cannot go wrong putting your own thoughts down on paper and formulating a quality laid out story that you may have been wanting to get out to the world and haven't known how! WOW is right! I wish I could have had a guideline like this for me to use as I wrote my first book. I will most definitely be applying all she is educating on in this book to my next project which is half complete. I will be going back and adjusting things accordingly so it is laid out in the best format possible for my next work to be a great success! Thank you Susie for your knowledge, for your sharing, for caring about how others put themselves out there to show up as the best version of themselves for their field of expertise! 3 Thumbs Up for an amazing guideline that will take you to the top as an expert as you write your compelling story or guidebook for your own industry!"
~ **Heather Pich,** Mentor and Trainer at Productive Learning,
#1 Bestselling Author of *Bookings When You Have No Bookings*

Writing to **WOW!**

to **WOW!**

BOOK WRITING WORKBOOK

SUSIE AUGUSTIN

GET
BRANDED
PRESS

Copyright © 2015 Susie Augustin

All rights reserved.
No portion of this book may be reproduced mechanically, electronically, or by any other means, including photocopying, without written permission of the publisher. It is illegal to copy this book, post it to a website, or distribute it by any other means without permission from the publisher.

Get Branded Press
Huntington Beach, CA 92648
www.GetBrandedPress.com

Limits of Liability and Disclaimer of Warranty.
The author and publisher shall not be liable for your misuse of this material. This book is strictly for informational and educational purposes.

Warning – Disclaimer.
The purpose of this book is to educate and entertain. The author and/or publisher do not guarantee that anyone following these techniques, suggestions, tips, ideas, or strategies will become successful. The author and/or publisher shall have neither liability nor responsibility to anyone with respect to anyone with respect to any loss or damage caused, or alleged to be caused, directly or indirectly by the information contained in this book.

ISBN 978-0-9770018-9-7 paperback

Library of Congress Cataloging-in-Publishing Data is available upon request.

Printed in the United States of America
First Printing, 2015

Cover & Interior Design by Kate Korniienko-Heidtman
Back Cover Photography by David Carlson

This book is dedicated to those of you who
Have always dreamed about writing a book.
I'm here to help you every step of the way.
Don't wait until you have all the
Skills and answers to get started.
Start where you are today.
Make it happen!

And for those of you who are
Writing a book to help brand your business,
This may be one of the
Best investments you make!

Dare to Wow the World with your Book!

ACKNOWLEDGMENTS

Writing to Wow! started out as a Book Writing Workshop that I created for entrepreneurs to help them brand themselves with their writing. I received many requests for additional services, so I created *Writing to Wow!* programs which include book coaching, editing, book cover, layout, and publishing. I knew from the beginning that I also wanted to offer a fun and fabulous hands-on workbook to help others get started on writing their books, and developed *Writing to Wow! Book Writing Workbook.*

Special thanks goes out to my *Writing to Wow!* Authors for taking a chance and putting their books in my hands to help guide them along the way:
Claudia Cooley – *Savyy Women Revving Up for Success* and *The 7 Mind Shifts*
Tracy Rath – *Louse Out: Every Kid's Self-Help Guide to the 11-Day Process of Getting Head Lice Out of Their Hair!*
Elizabeth Rosado-McGrath – *From Burned Out to Fired Up: Teachers Reignite Their Passion to Inspire*
Charles Nguyen – *How to Fund the College of Your Dreams*
Karla Keene – *Your Esthetics Coach*

To Kate Korniienko-Heidtman, my graphic designer, my deepest gratitude. My fabulous book covers and branding are contributing to the growth of Get Branded Press and *Writing to Wow!* I'm also grateful that you're helping my clients gain brand recognition with beautiful book covers, creative inside book layouts, and eye-catching social media graphics.

To Kim Somers Egelsee, thank you for your ongoing support of *Writing to Wow!* and for encouraging me to create the program, write the book, and expand my services. We've worked on a several books together already, and I envision many more in the future!

A special thank you to those who contributed their support, writing tips and more: Chris Widener for the foreword you provided and for being an inspiration; Kim Somers Egelsee and Nancy Ferrari for Visualization Exercises and tips; Marilyn Scott-Waters, Claudia Cooley, Karla Keene, Tracy Rath, Liz Rosado-McGrath, Heather Pich, Jackie Barros VanCampen, Buddy Sampson, and Kyle Wilson and Lessons From Experts.

Thanks to my girls for your friendship, inspiration, love and laughter: Shaeny, Kaylee, Danielle, Taylor Doll, Shirley, Kim, Claudia, Karla, Tashi, Stephanie, Kristen *and more!*

TABLE OF CONTENTS

FOREWORD

Would you like to write a book but are unsure of how to get started? Are you interested in taking your brand or business to another level by having a published book that reinforces your credibility? The book you have in your hands will help you reach these goals, with easy step-by-step activities that will help you choose your book topic and stay focused during the writing experience. Everyone gets writer's block at one time or another, and *Writing to Wow! Book Writing Workbook* provides tips and tools to open up your creativity, visualize your new book, discover why you want to share your experiences, and find techniques to overcome writer's block while you get your book written.

I first met Susie Augustin when I was invited to be the Keynote Speaker at *Living Your Extraordinary Life* Red Carpet Book Launch two years ago. This was a celebration for Susie's book *Sexy, Fit & Fab at Any Age!*, Kim Somers Egelsee's book *Getting Your Life to a 10 Plus*, and Claudia Cooley's *From Dud to Stud: Revving Up for Success*.

During this visit, I discovered that the book I wrote with Jim Rohn *Twelve Pillars*, is a favorite among these women. In addition, they mentioned that they preferred the compact 100 page size, which inspired them to write 100 page books themselves – the perfect length to contain enough content to make a difference, but not too intimidating – these days everyone seems to have short attention spans with the surge of smart phones, texting, and social media. This is also an ideal length of book for a first time author, and makes hitting a 10,000 – 20,000 word count more manageable.

Being a professional writer herself, Susie had questions for me about my writing experience, not only as an author, but as a ghostwriter. I have written 12 books and over 400 articles, and have been the "voice" for some of the biggest influencers in personal development. I'm delighted to be a mentor for other authors and entrepreneurs.

I'm pleased to know that I was there for Susie and the rest of these women during their journey, and am proud to see how far they've come. Each of these women are bestselling authors and passionate about what they share. They have definitely embraced the teachings of *Twelve Pillars*, which can be seen in how they help others around them succeed. Susie is a wonderful example of someone who creates her own opportunities and does not let obstacles stand in her way. She has clearly branded herself through her writing. I'm proud to be an influence and mentor.

Chris Widener is a seasoned businessman, a bestselling author, coach and consultant to CEOs and other C-level executives, as well as a dynamic speaker recognized worldwide. Author of over 400 articles and twelve books, Chris has produced more than 85 audio programs on the subjects of leadership, influence and motivation. He can be found on the web at www.ChrisWidener.com

INTRODUCTION

I'm so excited to help you write your book! It's amazing that you have the courage to go for it. Writing a book can be fun, scary, exciting, stressful – you will experience a roller coaster of emotions. If you don't, you may want to dare to go deeper...reveal more about yourself and add depth to your story.

I want to talk about *Writing Your Book to Brand Yourself* and what that means. I'll use myself as an example. I've been a Beauty and Branding Expert for 20 years, with an aesthetician's license and marketing degree. For decades I've been sharing my knowledge and experience with beauty professionals and their clients, discussing both inner and outer beauty. I've been working in the beauty industry as a marketing copywriter for several years with several multi-million dollar beauty brands, writing beauty copy, headlines and taglines, product names, packaging, displays, magazine ads, websites, blogs and social media.

All of my beauty and writing experience led to the creation of my Sexy, Fit & Fab™ brand. The first book uncovers the 8 keys to being *Sexy, Fit & Fab at Any Age!* including Spirit, Nutrition, Exercise, Education, Passion, Personality, Grooming, and Sex Appeal. This book reinforces my branding as a Beauty Expert – the go-to person for everything beauty.

My love for books and experience in writing, editing and proofreading was the perfect springboard for starting my own publishing imprint Get Branded Press. I originally started it so that I could publish my own books, but in the process I also edited and published my friend Kim Somers Egelsee's book *Getting Your Life to a 10 Plus*. Already a professional writer, this experience helped brand me as a Writing Expert. My *Writing to Wow!* programs strengthen my message – developing this workbook establishes me as the go-to person for questions on how to write a book, how to structure a book, how to self-publish a book, how to become a bestselling author.

Think about others you may know who have strengthened their brands when they've written a book. Did it give the impression that they were a credible professional in their field? Did they appear to have more knowledge than their competition? Did it bring them more business, speaking engagements and press?

Now think about yourself and your own positioning. How will your book help brand you? Is it related to your industry or career? Will it make others see you as an expert in your field? Will it reveal your hobbies, or perhaps that you're a compassionate person that wants to help others?

I challenge you to think BIG! You are an expert, an authority in your industry, you have years of experience to share that will help others in their journey to success.

WRITE YOUR BOOK TO BRAND YOURSELF

"How to have confidence in writing...Express your authentic, unique and most passionate self, unedited. Next review and edit anything that doesn't seem to flow. Finally, read it and make sure it matches you, your brand, and your topic."
~ Kim Somers Egelsee, *Confidence Expert*
#1 Bestselling Author of Getting Your Life to a 10 Plus

Having a published book is a fabulous way to brand yourself and your business. Are you a beauty expert, doctor, real estate agent, business coach, or holistic healer? Then this is the book for you. Did you know that books and ebooks are on the rise with entrepreneurs? A book that provides useful information is a valuable marketing tool, helping to promote and effectively brand your business. This increases your visibility, providing you with a new product to share in blog articles, newsletters, E-blasts, press releases, website and social media.

REPURPOSE YOUR MARKETING MATERIALS

Unsure of what to write about or stressing out over how to find the time and resources to create new content? If you are writing a book that correlates with your career or industry, you can repurpose your existing marketing materials. If you've already invested in developing a strong brand presence, you'll have an easier time integrating your ideas, expertise and teachings. Providing the educational information your clients are seeking, thereby creating a level of trust. Writing a book with valuable content can help you and your brand become a trusted authority in your industry, increase credibility, introduce your brand to new clients, and strengthen relationships with existing clients.

Repurposing your existing marketing materials is a great way to get a head start in outlining your book and filling in the chapters with content. Your marketing materials should already include your brand story, mission, educational information, benefits that your brand or services offer, as well as useful tips. Consider turning your collection of blogs into a book!

Gather all your marketing materials together:
- Website
- Brochures
- Catalogs
- Blog Articles
- Newsletters & E-blasts
- Social Media

YOUR MOST VALUABLE CALLING CARD
IS A PUBLISHED BOOK

Using your book to promote your business and brand yourself is genius! Having a published book offers many benefits and can get you in doors easier. I refer to my book as "an expensive business card", and at this time I give away more books than I sell. This is a marketing strategy, as well as a business write-off. Giving away copies of my books is a non-threatening way of opening up conversations about my books, brands and services, and has brought me more business than if my focus was strictly on selling copies of my book. I'm able to connect with my associates and build rapport, discover more about their business, find out ways we can help each other, and increase my chances of receiving referrals.

Here are some of benefits to having a published book:
- Creates buzz about your business
- Be seen as a leader in your field
- Become a trusted authority
- Score lucrative speaking engagements
- Connect with your target audience
- Fast track your success
- Attract higher paying clients
- Increase income with book sales
- Create multiple streams of income
- Strengthens brand recognition

In this hands-on workbook, you will find a topic to write about, name your book, outline your book, write your table of contents, chapter titles and summary for each chapter. Learn how to promote your business, brand yourself and increase your credibility.

Published books can lead to amazing opportunities:
- Related Products and Services
- Ebooks and Audiotapes
- Seminars
- Teleclasses
- Consulting Packages
- Speaking Engagements
- Radio Interviews
- TV Shows
- Magazine Articles

LET'S GET BRANDED

What is the name of your business or brand?

_____

_____

_____

_____

What is your tagline?

_____

_____

_____

_____

What does your logo look like?

_____

_____

_____

_____

What are your brand colors?

_____

_____

_____

_____

What industry are you in?

_____

_____

_____

_____

What products or services do you offer?

_____

_____

_____

_____

Who are your customers?

_____

_____

_____

_____

What are frequently asked questions about your brand?

_____

_____

_____

_____

What benefits does your brand provide?

_____

_____

_____

_____

What is your brand story?

_____

_____

_____

_____

USE VISUALIZATION TO OPEN UP CREATIVITY

"I believe that visualization is one of the most powerful means of achieving personal goals."
~ **Harvey Mackay**, *New York Times #1 Bestselling Author*

Some of you may have known for years that you've wanted to write a book, or maybe your mom always told you that you're a natural storyteller, while others may have recently had a spark of an idea and have decided to go for it. Whichever category you are in, this workbook includes many writing exercises to help you in the writing and creative process. This chapter covers visualization.

Wanting to write a book is a great start, but can you see yourself writing a book? Writing can be difficult and challenging at times, and having something to visually focus on will help. Have you visualized the experience? What will you feel like holding the book in your hands? Proud? Excited? Thrilled beyond belief? Can you imagine what it would be like to have a book launch celebration with your friends, family and business associates there to hear you share about the making of your book, what inspired you, and the difference it will make? What will you look like and what will you be wearing? Who's in the audience? What does your book look like? Seeing your book cover does something magical, you'll experience a new fire and passion for your book!

"Visualization is daydreaming with a purpose."
~ **Bo Bennett**

VISUALIZATION EXERCISES

ENVISION YOUR BOOK COVER

Your book cover design is essential in conveying what your book is about. It needs to be visually appealing. It can be literal or symbolic. Color is also important and should be linked to your branding.

The process of creating a book cover is very important. I've witnessed some book covers taking months to create, while others have been done in a day. Being clear on what you want helps the process go smoothly. New to all of this book stuff and have no clue? Be sure your publisher or graphic designer can help you through the creative process. You don't want to settle for a book cover that is "just ok".

Really open up your creativity to visualize your book cover. See the design, the colors, your name on the book. Take some time and draw a picture of your book cover. You don't have to be an artist, stick figures are ok. If you can add color, do that too. Add your book title and your name. You may end up with a few different book cover drawings throughout the process of writing your book. Your ideas may evolve, and as you write, you may gain even more confidence. It's normal at first to be a little conservative, but as your book comes to life, you may become more daring and really be ready to establish yourself as an expert of this new fabulous book.

12 Susie Augustin

Draw or Write Front Book Cover Ideas

Draw or Write Back Book Cover Ideas

STRENGTHENING SELF-CONFIDENCE
by Kim Somers Egelsee

Visualize yourself sitting relaxed in a gorgeous serene location. You feel flowing and at ease in every way. As you see yourself in this beauty, you also feel amazing, look amazing and have your favorite things surrounding you; your favorite photos, flowers, items and objects.

As you sit in this beauty, you see a bright shining radiant *blue light* surrounding you. It starts to sweep over and within your whole body. This *blue light* magically and powerfully cleanses away any negativity within you about yourself, your life, your abilities and your talents. It fills in the knowingness and certainty that you have power, confidence, talents, abilities, positivity and self-esteem. You are filled with self-acceptance, self-appreciation, self-love, self-awareness and self-esteem. This *blue light* emotionally uplifts, encourages and supports you.

Now physically feel the warmth of this magnificent *blue light* around you, within you and your being. Feel the love it brings. It cleanses away all insecurities, negativity, doubt and uncertainties. It leaves the power within so that you will always, from this moment on, have powerful fulfilling confidence and self-esteem, giving you continuous certainty and positive power. Any time you need this extra confidence boost, feel the warmth of this *blue light* within.

You now realize that your self-love and confidence have always been there in its fullness. The *blue light* just cleansed away some of the blocks. Your self-love and acceptance becomes more powerful daily. You love yourself and others, and this radiates from your being naturally from now on. Positive people and opportunities now flow to you constantly, easily and effortlessly. You have certainty about your talents and abilities. You are able to help others more freely with this new power and confidence. You look forward to every day, because you now have your full positive power flowing forth from you, radiating and attracting positivity. You look, feel and are greatness! Confidence! Power! Love!

Write Positive Power Words That Describe How You Feel

_____

_____

_____

_____

_____

_____

_____

_____

_____

_____

_____

_____

_____

_____

_____

_____

_____

_____

_____

_____

WRITING RITUAL
by *Nancy Ferrari*

Writing is one of the most sacred forms of creative expression for me. When I am in my creative flow and inspiration floods my mind, my pen writes my thoughts effortlessly. However, there are times when the flow is at a standstill. That's when I shift into my *Visionary Mindset* and imagine a gentle flowing river. As I envision the river and the pretty pebbles under the water, I see a boulder a few feet downstream. Now I can see why I am feeling a blockage from my free flow writing ability. I proceed to wade into the river and move the boulder off to the side, feeling an instant sense of joy as the water is in motion again. I'm now elated as my creative energy is free flowing once again and feel very inspired to write to my heart's content.

What Type of Visuals Represent Creative Flow for You?

_____
_____
_____
_____
_____
_____
_____
_____
_____
_____
_____
_____

CHOOSE YOUR TOPIC

For some of us, our book topics may be obvious. For example, you are a success coach and want to write a book about *The Top 10 Tips to Success*. For others, choosing the topic of your book can be daunting. You may have the spark within you, but maybe not the confidence to tell the world that you are an expert. You may have been raised to believe that it's more humble to stay in the background, or that it's selfish to take center stage. Getting clear on who you are and the unique talents you offer can get you closer to discovering what message you want to share with the world.

Still unsure?
Answering the following questions may help you focus.

Are you living your passion?

_____
_____
_____
_____

Have you positioned yourself as an expert?

_____
_____
_____
_____

Do you want to enhance your credibility?

_____
_____
_____
_____

WHAT ARE YOU PASSIONATE ABOUT?

Ask Yourself the Following Questions:

What is your expertise?

_____

_____

_____

What are you passionate about?

_____

_____

_____

What are your hobbies?

_____

_____

_____

What industry are you in?

_____

_____

_____

What makes you an expert?

_____

_____

_____

What are your unique talents?

_____
_____
_____

What makes you different?

_____
_____
_____

What do you offer?

_____
_____
_____

What are the benefits of your products, services, knowledge?

_____
_____
_____

What difference do you want to make with this book?

_____
_____
_____

What is your story?

_____
_____
_____

What brought you to your passion, business, or industry?

_____
_____
_____

What challenges or difficulties did you meet or overcome?

_____
_____
_____

What steps did you take?

_____
_____
_____

What is the significance of your contribution?

_____
_____
_____

Topic Suggestions
- Steps to Success
- Stories of Inspiration
- Beauty from the Inside Out
- Marketing Toolbox
- Success in Social Media
- Vegan Inspired Living
- How to Hit a Home Run Every Time

WHY ARE YOU WRITING A BOOK?

Being connected to and aware of your WHY will help keep you going when you feel discouraged, get writer's block, and face everyday life challenges.

Ask yourself the following questions. When you are answering the questions, really visualize this happening for you. What would it look like and feel like? Write down your answers.

Why are you writing this book?

_____
_____
_____
_____
_____
_____
_____
_____

What will the experience of writing be like?

_____
_____
_____
_____
_____
_____
_____
_____

What does it feel like knowing you are going to be a published author?

_____

_____

_____

_____

_____

_____

What benefits will it bring you? *Credibility, brand awareness, speaking opportunities, articles, radio & TV interviews, a feeling of accomplishment.*

_____

_____

_____

_____

_____

_____

What will it feel like if you don't get your book written? *What will you feel like, what opportunities do you think will not be available?*

_____

_____

_____

_____

_____

"Writing can be draining. Sometimes you wonder why you are so compelled. It is what you are. Allow it. Even if it is only for yourself."
*~ **Tracy Rath**, #1 Bestselling Author of Louse Out*

OUTLINE YOUR BOOK

Outlining your book will help you organize your topics, thoughts and ideas. Doing an outline will help you create your book in sections. It will help you focus on your overall topic, as well as focus on the separate sections of the book.

Is there a right way to organize your book? A wrong way? There are several different ways to organize, construct and write your book, and you will be offered different techniques to find what works best for you. You may feel that trying a combination of the different techniques provides you with the best results.

I know a few friends/authors who are gifted with free flowing creativity; the story comes right out of them. This is a rare find, and I've had the pleasure of working with speakers and brand managers who have this talent. It makes my job easier in editing and organizing material that already has the creativity built in.

As for myself, I'm a professional marketing copywriter in the beauty industry. I write websites, brochures, catalogs, packaging, social media, blogs and more for some of the top beauty brands out there. I take on an organized approach. I first like to know what format I'm writing for – website, packaging, brochure, etc. Then I want to know how much space is allowed – 1 sentence, 3 sentences, a paragraph, a whole page, etc. What style is the writing – marketing copy, educational, paragraphs, bullet points? Once I have the formatting information I need, I do my research. I look at existing brand information, competitor information, and online research. I then narrow down the research and apply it to the requested format. I ensure that the information is correct. Once that is complete, I add creativity and marketing copy. I edit, proofread and finesse, as well as look for consistency and flow. Taking on this approach can be tough, and I really have to trust the process. As the majority of the creativity isn't added until the end, what I'm working on can appear boring and very "textbook like". It can feel a little painful, and look a little hopeless. But it feels fabulous as I get into my zone and the creativity flows out of me, and I remember why I have a passion for writing.

Let's get started on creating a book outline. Some of you will be able to complete it effortlessly, while others may be able to fill in part of the information – it may take more time and research to complete it. Don't worry about making it perfect the first time. Writing down ideas and key words are just fine.

Afterward, you'll transfer the information into a diagram. Sometimes seeing your content in a different format can help the creative juices flow.

OUTLINE

Your book will include an overall topic with several sections and subsections. It can be difficult trying to figure out how to get started. The Book Outline activities include the basics to keep you focused. This is the most important part of getting your book written, and deciding what content to include and expand on.

- Topic/Name of Book
- Chapter Titles
- Subchapters

Unsure of where to start?
Think Keys, Tips, Lessons, Steps, Secrets

During the creation of your manuscript, you can keep in mind the other sections you'll need to add later on.

- Testimonials
- Foreword
- Introduction
- Table of Contents
- Acknowledgments
- Dedication
- Copyright Page
- About the Author
- Contact Info
- Back Cover Info

Topic / Name of Book

_____

Write down your Chapter Titles (5-10 Subjects)

1.

_____

2.

_____

3.

_____

4.

_____

5.

_____

6.

_____

7.

_____

8.

_____

9.

_____

10.

_____

Write Down Your Chapter Titles (5-10 Subjects)
Write Down Your Subchapters (3-5 sections per Chapter)

1.
   a. _____
   b. _____
   c. _____

2.
   a. _____
   b. _____
   c. _____

3.
   a. _____
   b. _____
   c. _____

4.
   a. _____
   b. _____
   c. _____

5.
   a. _____
   b. _____
   c. _____

6.

   a. _____

   b. _____

   c. _____

7.

   a. _____

   b. _____

   c. _____

8.

   a. _____

   b. _____

   c. _____

9.

   a. _____

   b. _____

   c. _____

10.

   a. _____

   b. _____

   c. _____

DIAGRAM

Write down your Topic/Name of Book in the center

Write Chapter Title on each line (5-10)

Write Subchapter in each box (3-5)
OK to use bullet points

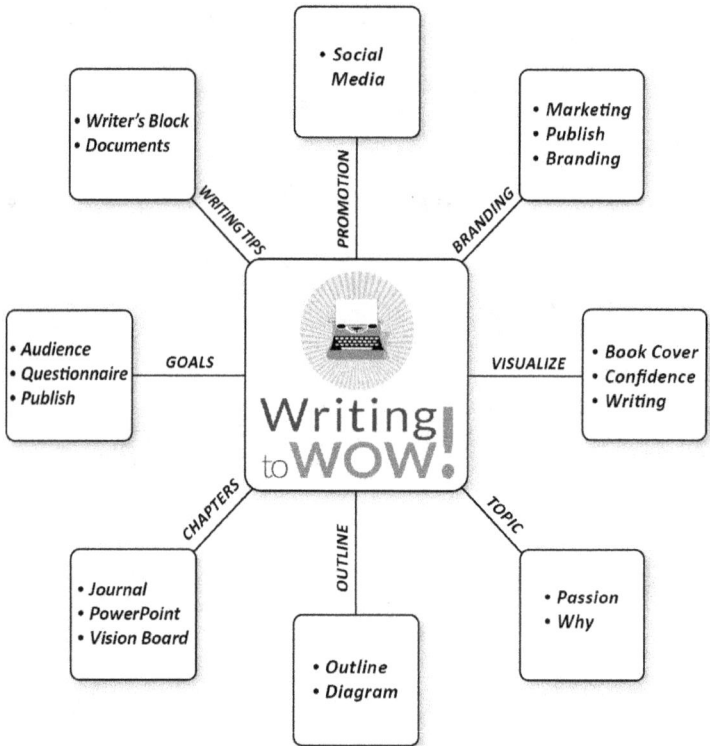

* Social
  Media

* Writer's Block
* Documents

* Marketing
* Publish
* Branding

WRITING TIPS

PROMOTION

BRANDING

* Audience
* Questionnaire
* Publish

GOALS

VISUALIZE

* Book Cover
* Confidence
* Writing

Writing!
to WOW!

CHAPTERS

OUTLINE

TOPIC

* Journal
* PowerPoint
* Vision Board

* Passion
* Why

* Outline
* Diagram

EXAMPLE of *Writing to Wow!* Outline

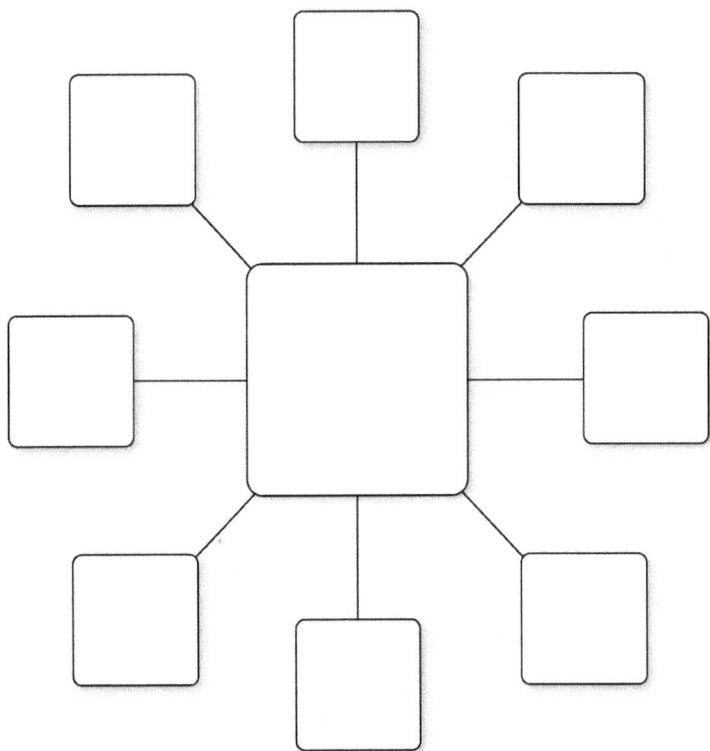

DEVELOPING CHAPTERS
AND SUBCHAPTERS

JOURNALING

"Set the mood of the place where you will write. I need quiet, I need comfortable. I make some notes ahead of time as to what I want to cover. As I begin, it's almost like journaling. I go in and let it flow out of me. Then, I come back to it later and start organizing it more and rephrasing. I like to do things in steps. I like to write in steps. It's the way I learn, and I feel a lot of others learn that way too."
~ ***Heather Pich***, *#1 Bestselling Author of Bookings When You Have No Bookings*

You may want to establish some writing habits or rituals before you jump into "writing the book" to take some of the pressure off, as well as open up your creativity. My most beneficial habit is journaling. I strive to journal every day in a notebook, writing 1-3 pages. Yes, writing with a pen, not typing into your laptop. Let your thoughts flow. If you're feeling negative or mad about life situations, let it all out. Be sure to then follow up your negativity with some positivity. Write a list of what you're grateful for. If you're going through tough times, you can write, "I'm grateful for my cat" or "I'm thankful for my new shoes." Mainly, I do stream of consciousness writing. Doing this daily will help you in releasing negativity, obsessive thoughts, and open up your creativity. Draw or doodle. You may get book ideas or marketing ideas. I like to draw pictures of myself speaking in front of an audience about my book. Of course I have amazing hair, am wearing a sexy dress, and look very happy. Seeing something like this brings me excitement, and helps me push through the challenges of writing and of life.

While journaling, don't worry about being articulate or creating a masterpiece. My notebooks are so filled with scrawled writing and scribbles, no reference to me being a "writer." Writing by hand helps with the cognitive process. It's a more natural way of writing down thoughts and ideas. I love reading about professional writers who buy Moleskin notebooks and fountain pens for their writing – how romantic! Something that special would slow down my writing, though. I don't want to scrawl all of my ideas in something so fancy. For my own personal writing, I like cheap notebooks and hotel pens (you know, the free ones you get at events and conferences?) For professional writing, I like to use legal pads and ballpoint pens. I also keep manila folders with printouts of what I'm working on.

In a notebook, write whatever comes to mind. Don't judge yourself or worry about spelling or grammar. That can be fixed later. Writing without judgment or trying to be perfect helps you open up. Write it all down. As your thoughts start coming together on paper, type your thoughts, ideas and writings into a Word doc and print it out. You may find that you only have a little information, or even too much. Get it all down.

During this process, it's good to also do some research. Find what you can on your topic, take notes, and buy books that are similar to what you want to write about. You do not want to copy or steal ideas, but it's helpful to see what information is similar to yours, as well as what viewpoints conflict with yours. Hopefully, this will give you confidence that you are right on track, as well as know that what you have to offer and the style you communicate with is unique.

There are many options and methods you can use to move forward. You choose what works best for you. Some like to work chronologically. Others choose to work on the creative or more fun sections. Most manuscripts will have a least one chapter that's deep, revealing, and difficult to write. You can dive right in and write that first, or breeze through the rest of your manuscript and tackle the difficult sections last.

As your writing progresses, transfer the information we went over in the previous chapter (outlining your book, chapter title, subchapters, etc.) into a Word doc. Organize your thoughts and writings into the separate sections. There is no right or wrong way of doing this. You can have one long running document, or several small documents with individual chapters. I will typically start with smaller individual documents, and as I get closer to completion, I'll create one large document.

Be sure to save your work as you write. Especially as you edit. Sometimes you accidentally press the wrong button, your cat jumps on your keyboard, or your computer locks up, and then you have to go back and recreate what you've already written. This usually happens once or twice on each project I work on. Not fun.

"Your first draft will be flawed, awkward, bad, horrible, embarrassing and a hundred other things that you haven't experienced since junior high...soldier on. Hunker down and keep writing until you get to the end, then revise and refine."
~ **Marilyn Scott-Waters**, *Award-Winning Illustrator and Author of The Toymaker*

As your work comes together and you're putting all the pieces together, or as writer's block kicks in and you wonder what ever possessed you to think you could be a writer or tackle such a big project, the time will come that you should consider printing out your manuscript. Particularly when you are ready to edit, you'll want to read off a printed page, rather than just the computer screen. You will notice things that you didn't see before. Grammar, spelling, punctuation, sentence structure and style will stand out more.

Print out your manuscript, get a pen, and start reading out loud. Reading out loud will help you hear if your sentences are choppy or awkward, or if you are repeating words or adjectives. Underline or circle these sections or words. It's easiest to allow yourself to just be free flowing with ideas and writing, without worrying about getting everything correct; you can go back with your edited manuscript and spend some time with Thesaurus.

When final edits are complete, celebrate with a glass of wine and bowl of mac & cheese!

When You Hear the Word "Journaling" What Comes to Mind? *Do you have positive or negative connotations? You can think of it as a place to express thoughts, feelings and ideas.*

_____

_____

_____

_____

_____

_____

_____

_____

_____

_____

_____

_____

_____

_____

_____

_____

_____

_____

_____

_____

_____

_____

_____

_____

_____

_____

_____

CREATE A POWERPOINT PRESENTATION

"Create your book or section of your book in PowerPoint slides. This really helps with getting the big ideas nailed down."
~ Liz Rosado-McGrath, MEd, *Author* of *From Burned Out to Fired Up: Teachers Reignite Their Passion to Inspire*

Creating a PowerPoint Presentation will help you outline your book, visualize your topic and content, and may contribute to your branding.

- Choose a template. I like a plain template that I can add visuals to, which will drive the look. You can also add your branding colors.
- Choose a font and font size that are easy to read. Helvetica and Arial are easy on the eyes. Scripts can be distracting.
- Use bullet points or short sentences.
- Add graphics or visuals.
- Practice your PowerPoint presentation as if you were speaking to a person or audience (this will help you develop your story).
- What would you talk about?
- What stories would you tell?
- Say it out loud.
- Add examples and quotes.

Visuals help, as you can get a clear picture of what your story or theme is all about, and it may reveal what you've left out.

STORYBOARDS & VISION BOARDS

"Create a storyboard with Post-it notes showing the rise and fall of the story. Remember that your story should have three acts:
1. Beginning, asking questions and getting the reader hooked.
2. Middle, keeping them reading.
3. Third act, tying everything up in a satisfying end."
~ **Marilyn Scott-Waters**, *Award-Winning Illustrator and Author of The Toymaker*

Just as powerful as developing a PowerPoint is creating storyboards and vision boards. The storyboard can be specific to your actual book, and can be as brief or complex as you want it to be. It will help with establishing your categories, finding which sections go together, and it's a nice visual way to move around and rearrange the different sections of your book.

What are the Different Sections of Your Book?

_____

_____

_____

_____

_____

_____

_____

_____

_____

_____

A vision board is another fabulous way of keeping a visual representation of not only your book, but also you as an author, speaker and expert. What you'll need: a fabulous picture of yourself, a picture of your book cover, a piece of thick paper (8.5x11 is fine) and a stack of magazines (or find images online). Start with doing one of the visualizations in this workbook, then select pictures, images and words that connect with how you envision the impact you will make with your book. Glue or tape them onto your piece of paper. Not feeling crafty? Go online and select images, insert them into a PowerPoint slide, and rearrange them to create a powerful visual.

When you are feeling discouraged or too busy to write, take out your vision board to remind you WHY you are doing this. To keep the image in front of you to stay inspired, use it as your computer and phone screensavers.

What Images and Words Will You Add to Your Vision Board?

_____

_____

_____

_____

_____

_____

_____

_____

_____

_____

_____

SPEAK YOUR STORY
USE VOICE RECOGNITION SOFTWARE

Are you a natural storyteller? Do you have free flowing ideas that you love to communicate? Is one of your sentences the length of a typical paragraph? Are you a speaker, and already have an arsenal of speeches? Did you roll your eyes when I suggested that you get out a notebook and pen and start WRITING, journaling? Then voice recognition software may be the solution for you. There are many available that you can use on your smart phone, tablet, laptop, desktop, and don't forget to check out the latest apps. Do some research, read reviews, and find the one that will work best for you. You'll want one that is more than just a recorder. Get one that will also type up your dictation. This may also be the solution for you if you are uncomfortable with the writing process. You can ask a friend to interview you, so your thoughts come out naturally and free flowing.

I haven't actually used voice recognition software yet. It's available on my laptop, but writing by hand is still my favorite method of writing. I enjoy the writing process. I purchased a tablet a year ago, with the intention of using it for a future project where I'll be interviewing contributing authors. I'll probably get an app 5 minutes before I start that project.

The benefits of using voice recognition software is that it can catapult someone's story that may not have otherwise been written. I also heard that it can be a great timesaver.

DETERMINE YOUR GOALS

What are your goals for writing your book? Is it to teach others specialized information, or for entertainment? Is it to use as a marketing tool and increase your business, to have a product to sell at your speaking engagements or events?

Go back to the section where you explored WHY you are writing your book. Here are some goals you may be considering:
- To create multiple streams of income
- To create visibility to land Speaking Engagements, TV spots, Radio interviews, Magazine articles
- To promote your business and brand yourself
- To gain credibility
- To make money selling books and products

What are Your Goals?

_____
_____
_____
_____
_____
_____
_____
_____
_____
_____
_____
_____
_____
_____
_____

KNOW YOUR AUDIENCE

Knowing your audience is an important aspect to writing when it comes to style, tone, length, layout and information included. Is this book for the masses or for a specific industry? Who will benefit from your book and why? Is it educational? Will you include how-to steps? Or will it be told in storyteller fashion and include humor?

Who is this book for?

_____

What is the age range?

_____

What gender is it for? Men, women, children?

_____

Is this a book for moms or momtrepreneurs?

_____

A specific industry?

_____

The Manuscript Questionnaire will help you gain even more clarity. Another benefit of it is that it will help you articulate the details of your book (why you are writing it and who it is for) when you have conversations with colleagues, agents, publishers, designers, and others who may end up helping you in some capacity with your book.

MANUSCRIPT QUESTIONNAIRE

1. Book Title and Subtitle (include several ideas and variations):

_____

_____

_____

_____

2. Author Name (how you want it to appear on book cover):

_____

_____

_____

_____

3. Are you the only author of the book, or will you be crediting additional author/authors? Will they be listed on the front or back cover?

_____

_____

_____

_____

4. What is your job/position/career?

_____

_____

_____

_____

5. What is your book topic?

_____

_____

_____

_____

6. List 5-10 keywords that correlate to your book topic:

_____

_____

_____

_____

7. Book Chapters and Subchapters:

_____

_____

_____

_____

8. Write a brief description of your book (this may appear on your back book cover):

_____

_____

_____

_____

9. What books are similar in subject or industry? How will your book be original or different?

_____

_____

_____

_____

10. What will your audience gain from reading your book?

_____

_____

_____

_____

11. WHY are you writing this book? What is your passion behind it? What do you hope to gain personally and professionally?

_____

_____

_____

_____

12. Author biography (in one paragraph, write your relevant expertise and credentials):

_____

_____

_____

_____

13. What length book would you like to write? (100 or 150 pages?) What is the length of your manuscript? (10,000 or 20,000 words?)

_____

_____

_____

_____

14. Target Market – who is the audience for your book, and what is their age range?

_____

_____

_____

_____

15. Who will write your foreword?

_____

_____

_____

_____

16. Will you include an introduction?

_____

_____

_____

_____

17. Who would you like to obtain endorsements/testimonials from (that are relevant to your subject or industry)?

_____

_____

_____

_____

18. What is your goal for this book? (brand recognition, educate your clients, make a difference, make money)

_____

_____

_____

_____

19. Will your book include activities, notes, or tips?

_____

_____

_____

_____

20. Are there professional organizations or a certain industry who may buy your book in large quantities?

_____

_____

_____

_____

21. Are there organizations, industries or groups who you may want to donate your book to?

_____

_____

_____

_____

22. Does your book train any groups or industries?

_____

_____

_____

_____

23. Are there any other goals, objectives, or thoughts you have about your book that you would like to share?

_____

_____

_____

_____

24. How will you promote and market the book (speaking, blog, website, social media, giveaways, mailing list, newsletter)?

_____

_____

_____

_____

25. What is your marketing strategy and selling points for your book?

_____

_____

_____

_____

26. Are there industry professionals or publications that you would like to review your book?

_____

_____

_____

_____

27. Who are industry experts, friends, contacts who may help you promote your book?

_____

_____

_____

_____

28. Have you written articles or have you been interviewed on your topic or industry?

_____

_____

_____

_____

29. Are you interested in speaking about the topic of your book?

_____

_____

_____

_____

30. What audience/industry would you like to speak to?

_____

_____

_____

_____

31. Are you interested in being interviewed on radio or TV shows?

_____

_____

_____

_____

32. Are you going to write blog articles or magazine articles on your book or topic?

_____

_____

_____

_____

33. Do you view your book as being an investment, profitable, or both? Do you see yourself giving away books for marketing purposes and brand recognition, or selling at events, trade shows, and on your website?

_____

_____

_____

_____

34. Do you have an agent or publisher?

_____

_____

_____

_____

35. Are you interested in being published or in self-publishing?

_____

_____

_____

_____

36. Are you interested in learning about self-publishing?

_____

_____

_____

_____

PUBLISHING vs SELF-PUBLISHING

How many of you have fantasized or daydreamed about being discovered for your unique talents and becoming a published author? Of being invited to be a guest speaker and making bundles of money? Of sitting on the beach while your screenplay is being filmed, counting your royalty checks that are rolling in? These can be great stimulations to get your book written, as long as you are willing to actual do the WRITING! However, most of us are driven by the content or story we want to share, and have this burning desire to make it happen – with or without the awards or recognition they may bring us.

There's nothing quite like the feeling of finishing your manuscript and dreaming of getting published. But you need to be aware of what you are getting into. You'll want to do some research and find writing workshops to attend, as well as writing conferences. These are a lot of fun and you will acquire so much information from authors, illustrators, designers, agents and publishers. Absorb the information and take notes. You will want to pay a little extra to get an interview with an agent and publisher. They may advise you on your manuscript, or even your next steps. You may decide not to follow their advice, it's all part of the research process.

Listening to the speakers will give you insight – not only of the success of "making it", but also of the reality of what is involved – hard work, time, money, and other sacrifices. What always stood out the most to me was the time. For most, it can take six months to one year (or several years) to write your manuscript. Then it may take the same amount of time to impress an agent enough to start pitching you to publishers. Once a publisher shows interest, there may be an additional year of editing. Once they feel your script has potential, they will design a cover and interior layout, and send the book overseas for printing. You will receive a small advance (unless you are a celebrity or have an established audience), a PR campaign will be created, and a book signing schedule for when the book is available in print six months later, if you are lucky. This entire process can take a few to several years.

After the research I conducted, I came to the conclusion that it takes approximately three years minimum to be published the traditional way. Which led me to be open-minded and listen to those who were sharing information about self-publishing. This was around 10 years ago. I'd written and illustrated a children's book about mermaids for my niece. I went to some conferences, and the agent and publisher I met with both told me the same thing: develop my story more, and make a decision if I want to write or illustrate, because no one will offer me a contract to do both. I was passionate about my project, and believe it or not, I was more into drawing and painting mermaids at the time than I was interested in writing. I did further research and filed a dba (Mermaid Studios), contacted Bowker and bought 10 ISBN numbers, as I planned on writing and illustrating a series of mermaid books. At that time, color printing was so expensive and out of the question. I scanned my illustrations and purchased an expensive printer, printed out the pages, and created handmade books.

I spoke to a few groups and had a booth at the Huntington Beach Art-a-Faire on the pier. It was a lot of fun, but it was also around the time that prefab art was becoming popular and inexpensive. Not many people were buying hand painted mermaid art. Add to that a bad marriage, divorce, and a downturn in the economy. I did what any smart girl would do – I came up with a new plan. I went back to school to get a marketing degree, rediscovered my passion for writing, and became a marketing copywriter in the beauty industry. I've worked as a brand manager, as well as worked with several brand managers, graphic designers, web designers, PR and social media. Being a marketing copywriter isn't just about writing fun and creative copy – part of the job is editing, proofreading, and being aware of what layouts work and why.

During this time, my friend Kim Somers Egelsee asked me to edit her manuscript *Getting Your Life to a 10 Plus* so that she could submit it to a few publishers she knew. She also asked me to speak to her women's group about Health, Beauty & Sex Appeal. I created a PowerPoint presentation and my topic was a big hit, with many women requesting a book. Always up for a challenge, I turned my speech and PowerPoint into a book – I was already halfway there with my content, I just needed to develop my stories.

Of course I planned on self-publishing, I already owned all those ISBN numbers! My new dba is Get Branded, so I changed my imprint from Mermaid Studios to Get Branded Press. Kim's contacts fell through and I offered to publish her book, too. As I was finishing up writing my book, I faced the hardest challenges in my life, all at once. I had a hysterectomy, my mom passed away, and I thought I was a victim of identity theft (I wasn't, the credit bureau combined me and another person, and the situation is still not fully resolved). In spite of my pain, I moved forward with our books (I had no credit or funds, so I did the inside book layouts myself). We had a fabulous book launch celebration with our friend Claudia Cooley, author of *From Dud to Stud: Revving Up for Success*, and Chris Widener was our Keynote Speaker. I changed the title of my book to *Sexy, Fit & Fab at Any Age!* and developed a strong look and presence for my book and brand – red, black and leopard. Our book launch celebration was a huge success with lots of support from family and friends. Kim did a small bestseller campaign, and her book hit #1 on Amazon! I was too focused on producing quality books to even think about any awards or accolades, so imagine my surprise when I returned home from the book launch at midnight and discovered that my book also hit bestseller! Thank you God! My book didn't hit #1, but it did reach #2, next to Jessica Alba's new book that took the #1 slot.

Since then, I wrote and published another *Sexy, Fit & Fab* book – *Sexy, Fit & Fab Sirens* (with 24 contributing authors) and I did a big bestseller campaign, hitting #1 in 17 categories! Next, I launched my *Writing to Wow!* six month program with five authors, including Claudia Cooley (*The 7 Mind Shifts* and *Savvy Women Revving Up for Success*). Get Branded Press did her editing, layout, book cover, and bestseller campaigns (Claudia has her own publishing imprint). Both books hit #1 bestseller and bestseller in several categories on Amazon – and her first book *From Dud to Stud: Revving Up for Success* hit #2 – two years after its release! In addition to mine and my clients' books becoming Amazon Bestsellers, they've also won awards including The Beverly Hills Book Awards and The International Book Awards. I'm excited to develop my next book *Sexy, Fit & Fab Beauty Secrets*, followed by *Sexy, Fit & Fab Studs*.

I'm thrilled that self-publishing and print-on-demand services have evolved in the past decade, making it affordable for more authors to self-publish. I researched different options, and the choice I made over two years ago is the same one I choose now. I use and recommend the services of CreateSpace, owned by Amazon. They have publishing services (ISBNs, etc.) but I recommend that authors purchase their own ISBN from Bowker/Identifiers. They also offer affordable layouts, cover designs, editing and ebook services, which I have not used at this time. I use CreateSpace as my print-on-demand and distribution source. Their website provides full information on their services and prices.

Should anyone self-publish? Anyone can, but I strongly suggest that you strive for quality – in content, layout and cover design. If you are a do-it-yourselfer, you owe it to your readers to conduct extensive research on how to develop and design it correctly, or hire professionals to help you. Nothing screams self-publishing more than a poorly edited book with a bad layout and bad cover. You must go online and go to bookstores, take a look at what's been done traditionally, as well as look at the books that are a little more unique.

Who should you hire to help you, and how much does it cost to write and publish a book? Once again, do your research. There are many vanity publishers that publish quality books. There's also a price. For full service, it costs approximately $10,000. Most also offer ala carte services. They can edit and publish your book, getting it print ready in under 12 months. Earlier, we covered traditional publishing and the number of years it takes (three years minimum). You need to look at writing and publishing your book as an investment. It takes a combination of time and money. Some of us pay less money, but put in thousands of dollars worth of time. Is it worth it? Sometimes during the writing process when it gets tough, you may question your decisions – I certainly do. Or when you run out of money to pay your bills because you've invested your savings in publishing and printing, you may wonder what possessed you to want to do this. Or when you realize you've become a hermit in order to finish your manuscript, and haven't been to an event in months. But then…you see your new book cover and layout, you upload your book for print, you're holding your new book in your hands, you've been promoting your book and it's hitting on Amazon, you're speaking at your book launch celebration and sharing your story…yes, it's worth it!

WRITING TIPS

OPEN UP CREATIVITY
AND BANISH WRITER'S BLOCK

Create writing rituals so that your brain knows it's time to get down to writing. It sometimes feels like avoidance, but many times you'll be surprised by new creative ideas.

- Journal every day in a notebook, get negative or obsessive thoughts out, letting your creativity flow
- Handwrite your ideas instead of typing them on the computer
- File and paint your nails
- Listen to "background music" – Salsa music in Spanish gets me in the mood
- Take a nature walk – on the beach, in the park, etc.
- Conduct more research; gets you into your subject and can spark new ideas
- Some days when you're feeling very resistant, you may end up with a very clean house or apartment, instead of chapters written
- When deadlines are looming, bribe yourself with pizza and wine
- Be willing to write crap – don't worry no one has to read it – eventually through the process of just writing anyway, the words will start to flow, allowing you to sound creative and articulate again
- Don't stress over a messy desk – in the middle of big projects, it may look like a hurricane hit – on your desk, your coffee table, and your nightstand
- Wear comfortable clothes, don't let the way you look interfere with your creativity

"When experiencing writer's block, create and continue to add to a gratitude list. This helps tap into a free flow of good feelings that can unblock energy that has become stuck."
~ **Liz Rosado-McGrath, MEd,** Author of From Burned Out to Fired Up: Teachers Reignite Their Passion to Inspire

"Sometimes music is my best friend during my writing time. But it has to be the kind of music that inspires my creative flow. I have it loud in my earpods and just let it drive my writing. It's awesome!"
~ **Jackie Barros VanCampen**, Author of Letters to My Daughter

"Add your sense of humor to your writing to connect with your readers on a more personal level."
~ **Karla Keene**, Author of Your Esthetics Coach

"First, clear your mind of all distractions. I love going to Malibu to write because the ocean and the waves coming in and out serves to clear my thoughts and make me creative."
~ **Buddy Sampson**, Publisher of The Scoop LA, Professional Musician

"When you are experiencing "writer's block", write down words while at the kitchen counter, at the stoplight, in the market. Feed your creativity. Suddenly, the words will flow."
~ **Tracy Rath**, #1 Bestselling Author of Louse Out

What Helps You With Writer's Block?

_____
_____
_____
_____
_____
_____
_____
_____
_____
_____
_____
_____
_____
_____
_____
_____
_____
_____
_____
_____
_____
_____
_____
_____
_____
_____
_____
_____

TIPS ON SAVING DOCUMENTS

During any writing projects, it's important to keep your documents organized, labeled with the date, and in relevant folders to keep track of your progress. This is especially important when you are working with another writer or editor. Nothing is worse than making extensive changes on the wrong document! Why do you want to keep your old versions? In case you accidentally erase or lose your newest version. Or, you may revise and make changes, but then change your mind about what you've changed. It's also a good idea to create and label a few other documents – "notes" and "research". Check with publisher for formatting specifics (incorrect formats may be rejected or sent back). If you write in Pages, save a version in Word format.

Creating Folders and Documents
- Create a new folder on your desktop and name it "Book" or "Manuscript"
- Save different versions of your documents with title, revision #, and date – *SusieBook rev2 6.1.15*
- Be sure you understand *Save* and *Save As* functions

Formatting Manuscript Basics
- Margins – 1" on all sides
- Standard Font and Size – Arial, Times New Roman or Courier in 12-point font size
- Single space is ideal while writing (but traditional publishers will require double spacing)

Add a Title Page, including Copyright © Year Name

TIME MANAGEMENT –
CREATE A WRITING SCHEDULE

"Allow yourself to be inspired. Set aside time for writing each week. I actually schedule the time on my calendar and give the time a special color. I usually set aside one day a week. Journaling is a great beginning, opening up ideas, and for inspiration to drop in. Definitely have a writing coach that keeps you on schedule once you are on the path of writing your book. I think it really helps to set a target date for your book to be published. Have FUN...this should be a very rewarding journey."
~ Claudia Cooley, *Bestselling Author/Speaker/Coach*

You've decided to write a book but are unsure of how to get started, and how often you should be writing. When do you want to finish your manuscript? When do you want your book print-ready? Creating a writing schedule and keeping to it can be a challenge. Even writer's block is minimal compared to other responsibilities and obligations:

- Family – Parents, Spouse, Kids
- Job/Work/Career
- Finances
- Friends and Social Life
- Fitness/Workout
- Nutrition
- Sleep & Relaxation
- Faith/Spirit
- Hobbies
- Grooming

Once again, it goes back to your WHY and what you are willing to give up to make room for this new project. What works for me may not work for you. I'm single and have two cats, which is entirely different from someone with a spouse and young kids. But just like anything in life, we adjust and make things happen. Life is a combination of responsibilities, priorities, and handling the curve balls that come our way.

There are several strategies, you may end up trying one or all of them, and decide which one works best for you.

- Mathematical – decide the size of book you want to write – how many pages, words, etc. and divide this into hours and days
- Quantity – binge writing – doing the bulk of your writing in long days or weekends, getting most of your word count out
- Create a spreadsheet with due dates and fill in the days you will write
- Writing rituals can lead into writing – journaling may create content
- Deadline is here – write it and write it fast
- Waiting to be inspired is a crapshoot
- Go to an all-inclusive day spa
- Write while on vacation
- Write at the beach
- Set up the perfect desk and atmosphere
- Write first thing in the morning
- Journal first thing in the morning
- Let your story "percolate" and then spend one day or a weekend getting it all on paper

What Kind of Schedule do You Feel Will Work Best for You and Why?

_____

_____

_____

_____

_____

_____

_____

_____

_____

_____

_____

_____

_____

_____

_____

_____

_____

_____

_____

_____

_____

_____

_____

_____

_____

_____

_____

"Respect the space, make your writing time a priority."
~ **Marilyn Scott-Waters**, *Award-Winning Illustrator and Author of The Toymaker*

Being a professional marketing copywriter, I trained myself to work within a *Timeline*, rather than a *Schedule*. I'm aware of the entire scope of the project, what parts of the project are due when, and determine when the copy or writing is due, while taking into consideration that edits will need to be done, too. Do I always feel inspired and really want to write? Is the environment always favorable? No and no. I trained myself to work within any environment – noisy, stressful, high intensity. Therefore, when I have the chance to go to a beautiful beach, writing is the last thing I want to do – I want to relax and read a book. I've trained myself to be a creative writer within very tight deadlines. But I've got to say, when it comes to your very own personal writing and stories – wow! Sometimes you feel naked and don't want to reveal yourself. You don't want to embarrass yourself or be criticized. It doesn't help that writing is such a journey, and many times the process does not produce interesting writing. There are very few people who I share my writing with while I'm in the process – just a few who I trust, and who realize they are being shown a rough draft, that are asked to give specific feedback (what's missing, what to add, remove, or change the order). Then I make those changes, print it out, do a full edit, and go back in and add in creativity, descriptions and better adjectives.

CREATING BOUNDARIES

Creating boundaries with family and friends while you are writing your book can at times be difficult, or faced with resistance. The best way to approach this is to have communication with your family – let them know what your book is about, why you are writing it, and the amount of time it may take. You may have to establish boundaries, schedules, and even barter and negotiate. I often have to bribe and reward myself during the writing process (especially as deadlines come closer). What are my bribes and rewards? Small ones to get immediate writing completed – pizza, wine, chocolate, a new novel. Bigger rewards for consistently meeting deadlines – new fabulous leopard dress for book launch. What can you negotiate with your spouse or family? Date night and new sexy lingerie, a trip to the beach or ballgame, movie night…?

You may have family members who are not supportive of your writing, and you may even be ridiculed. This is an important time for you to have strong faith, spirit, and read or listen to personal development books or CDs. You might make the decision not to share your writing goals with non-supporters or negative Nellies. You're going to have a hard enough time with all the "voices in your head" judging you. This may also be the time you pull away from friendships that are "barely tolerable" – you don't have to always be the "nice one", even if you are studying personal development (you'll be learning how to be strong and take care of yourself).

Some of your other close friends may take it personally and be hurt when you're unable to accept invitations or make commitments. Be creative! Most of you are writing your books to brand your business. Believe me, not everyone needs to know every detail of what you are doing. You may need to start saying with confidence, "I'm sorry, but I'll be working." This is not a lie or even an exaggeration. As your schedule gets more full, you will have to pick and choose what you will say "Yes" or "No" to. My friend Kim suggests, when faced with making a decision to accept or decline an invitation, ask yourself what percentage do you really want to do it? 10%? 50%? 80? If you don't want to do it at least 90% and it's not in alignment with your personal goals, then you shouldn't do it. Of course, there will be certain expectations and obligations that you really can't get out of.

Once again, having established writing rituals can be beneficial during these times, and can even help you tune out distractions and interruptions. Every so often I'll get ambitious – I'll be all set with a perfectly clean desk for writing time! The laptop gets turned on just as the gardeners below turn on the lawn mower or leaf blower. Lovely. Conducting a little extra research during such times never hurt anyone. Or how about when you are getting ready to do a final edit, and your neighbor chooses this time to blast her music? I just turn up my Spanish Salsa music!

Sometimes you have to pay attention to special cues from your pets (especially when you're on deadline, and they've been neglected). You've got to write something important, and that's when Kitty nudges your hand with his head – it's petting time! Best to just get the petting over with, as in a matter of minutes he'll be sprawled all over your papers, printouts and research. Or, when you've had several late nights in a row writing, and at bedtime he jumps onto your keyboard, curls up and goes to sleep… I take this as a sign to stop, have a glass of wine and watch some TV *(or go to bed!)* Anyone who has seen my social media pages may have seen pictures and documentation of Kitty's antics during production of my projects (and my clients' projects).

HOW TO CREATE LIFE BALANCE

Creating life balance while writing a book can feel impossible – you may have to choose to "stay in harmony" during this time of imbalance. Who can do everything? Something's gotta give – what will it be? This isn't always a conscious decision…what you initially start to neglect (nutrition, exercise, spirit, relationships, grooming, etc.) may end up taking the back burner long term. Again, out comes the negotiating, bribing, rewards – with yourself! Try not to give yourself too hard a time. But you may want to have a goal or come up with a plan and a timeline to get back in shape – I mean back in balance (did I say too much?) Yes, I'm a stress eater, and food and drink are also worked into my reward system.

LEARN TO COMPARTMENTALIZE

I've been asked several times how I'm able to write and publish my books in such a short time. I definitely have to make sacrifices, just like anyone else. I also know how to compartmentalize. I sometimes refer to it as "Think like a man." You know how women are sometimes referred to as broad minded and multi-taskers, while men are labeled as being single minded and super focused? I tend to compartmentalize a bit more than my female friends, but part of this process usually entails being less social and more in my head. I don't feel as obligated about certain things that most women do – I'm not sure if it's because I have seven brothers, am an Aries, am single with no kids...

Establishing writing habits and writing rituals will help you compartmentalize your writing time, allowing less distractions and interference.

What Factors do You Feel will Interfere with Your Writing?
What plan can you put in place to help you maintain a balanced life while your write your book?

_____
_____
_____
_____
_____
_____
_____
_____
_____
_____
_____
_____
_____
_____
_____
_____
_____
_____
_____
_____
_____
_____
_____
_____
_____
_____
_____

SHAMELESS
SELF-PROMOTION

Having a career in marketing and a love for everything branding, I've wanted to write a book about *Shameless Self-Promotion* for a few years now. I ended up switching gears and instead wrote *Sexy, Fit & Fab at Any Age!* I've been in the Beauty Industry for 20 years and I've worked with some of the hottest beauty brands out there, including L'Oreal Professional Hair Care, Bare Minerals, Salon Perfect, Ardell Lashes, and China Glaze nail polish.

It's acceptable for billions of dollars to be spent globally on marketing, PR and advertising, but many times there is criticism when the brand is a person – celebrities, actors, musicians, models, authors, speakers, etc. Why is this? We see a combination of love, hate, worship, envy, criticism and emulation. Those who are put on a pedestal are also likely to get pushed off it.

As an author, speaker and business owner, how can you promote yourself without receiving criticism? That's really not a practical way to approach your branding and promotion, as you can be the kindest person in the world living an unselfish life, and still the haters will come out. Being human, we will naturally feel the sting of insults, but we can't let the fear of how others will act or react, or how we imagine they'll act or react, drive our authentic selves.

Following your dreams and sharing your message with the world takes a lot of courage. Self-promotion is most effective when you start strengthening your brand – with your brand story, mission statement or tagline – with a look that's recognizable. Do you need to have all of your branding in place before you start promoting yourself or making appearances? Absolutely not! Continue moving forward with confidence, and work toward bringing everything together.

As you develop your brand, you want to work with a good designer to help you develop your look, and then take that look along with your brand message into your marketing materials — business cards, bookmarks, book covers, onesheets, brochures, website and social media. Be willing to show your authentic self. People are inspired not just by your success but also by your journey — the challenges and obstacles that you experienced and overcame, becoming stronger in the process.

When I use the term *Shameless Self-Promotion*, I use it in a very tongue-in-cheek way. It's an invitation to enjoy your brand while feeling confident and proud of yourself! For your personal brand, you'll want to mix it up a bit. Make sure you're aware of creating a balance of sharing your accomplishments with your real authentic self. Bring humanity to your brand and have a sense of humor.

For those of you that don't know me, I enjoy social media personally and love having this platform to share my brands. I'm grateful to have worked with some fabulous social media mavens in the beauty industry, and have learned so much! As my friend Kim first introduced me to social media, I asked her to contribute to this next section.

SOCIAL MEDIA STRATEGIES
by Kim Somers Egelsee

10 Strategies for Social Media – Confidence & Connecting

1. Business – Post about your business or brand and what you offer (products, services, coaching, etc.)

2. Personal – Show what's going on in your personal life... exciting trip, some news, family time, something you achieved.

3. Positive tips, affirmations or quotes (can be yours or from someone famous).

4. A Mix of Personal & Business.
Example:
I'm so happy I worked on my Ten Plus Life Coaching Certification today. I have many degrees that will add expertise to my Coaching business, too.

5. Plug or promote someone else and tag them.

6. Photos – Business or Personal.
Example:
Photos of you speaking, on the red carpet, on a trip, meeting with a client, having fun.

7. Media – Articles, Interviews, YouTube Videos, Radio or TV Shows.

8. Celebrate Acknowledgments – Awards, Certifications, Speaking, Activities that reflect your credibility.

Examples:

I'm so happy I'm halfway through my life coaching certification program.

Wow so amazing! I'm speaking in front of 50 people for a business today.

I'm honored and inspired to have my article featured on this blog. I just received an amazing testimonial about it.

9. Testimonials – Business, Coaching, Speaking, Writing, etc.

10. Questions – Ask a question and get your audience involved.

More Tips!

Messages: Ask, Sell, Connect!

Facebook Feed: Ask, ask, ask...

Branding, Sponsors, Strategic Partners.

SOCIAL MEDIA BRANDING

Do you have a business/brand page on social media?

_____

_____

_____

What are your unique hashtags?

_____

_____

_____

How often do you post?

_____

_____

_____

How are you interacting?

_____

_____

_____

Do you have contests or giveaways?

_____

_____

_____

Do you have anyone to cross-promote with?

_____

_____

_____

Have you successfully branded yourself on social media platforms?

_____

_____

_____

Remember that you will get more views, likes and comments when you include visuals. Be consistent in your brand look and message. Have fun and connect with your fans by mixing business, personal, accomplishments and humor. Interact with others to create a conversation.

LET'S CONNECT!

f 🐦 📷 g+

Facebook.com/GetBrandedPress
@GetBrandedPress
#GetBrandedPress
#WritingtoWow
#DreamitWriteitBrandit
www.GetBrandedPress.com

Facebook.com/SexyFitFab
@SexyFitFab
#SexyFitFab
#SexyFitFabSirens
#SexyCollaboration
www.SexyFitFab.com

To find out more about *Writing to Wow!* programs
or getting published with Get Branded Press,
contact Susie at **Susie@GetBrandedPress.com** or
www.**LinkedIn.com/in/SusieAugustin**

TO DOWNLOAD COPIES OF
BOOK OUTLINE WORKSHEETS AND DIAGRAM
go to *Writing to Wow!* downloads at
www.GetBrandedPress.com

ABOUT SUSIE AUGUSTIN

SUSIE AUGUSTIN inspires women of all ages to follow their passion, embrace their natural beauty and live a healthy lifestyle with her Sexy, Fit & Fab™ brand. She's the bestselling author of *Sexy, Fit & Fab at Any Age!*, *Sexy, Fit & Fab Sirens*, and upcoming *Sexy, Fit & Fab Beauty Secrets*. Susie's writing, speaking and publishing have garnered her Awards and Nominations including: Willow Tree Women's Circle "Extraordinary Woman Award"; Today's Innovative Woman "Innovative Woman of the Week" and "Success Summit Award"; Applaud Women Magazine "Inspirational Woman". *Sexy Fit & Fab at Any Age!* is a Beverly Hills Book Awards Winner (2014 Body/Mind/Spirit category and 2015 Beauty Category) and International Book Awards Finalist (Women's Issues). *Sexy Fit & Fab Sirens* is an International Book Awards Finalist (Self-Help/General).

Susie is a Beauty and Branding Expert (a Licensed Aesthetician with a Marketing Degree) and works as a marketing copywriter with some of the world's top rated beauty companies. She's a featured Marketing Expert for Applaud Women Magazine, a contributing author and on the national advisory board. To help others pursue their dreams and brand themselves through their writing, Susie created Get Branded Press, providing book coaching, editing, copywriting, publishing, and *Writing to Wow!* workshops. Her *Writing to Wow! Book Writing Workbook* will help reach a wider audience, guiding new authors to write books. Her mission for Get Branded Press is *Dream it. Write it. Brand it.*